conservation project book

Shirley Thompson and Phil Richardson

Illustrator Tessa Lovatt-Smith

Contents

The Bat Conservation Trust

Introducing you to bats

What kind of creature is it that flies with its hands, spends most of its time hanging upside-down and can find its way around in total darkness? The answer, of course, is a bat.

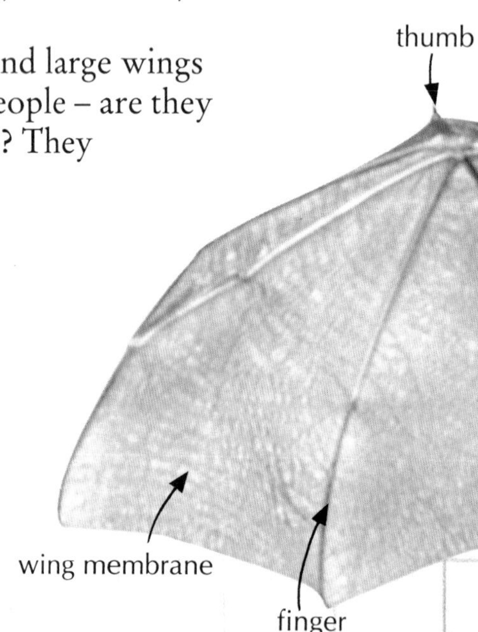

Bats' soft, furry bodies and large wings still sometimes confuse people – are they flying mice or furry birds? They are neither. Bats are mammals, as are mice, humans and other animals with hair or fur. Like all mammals, female bats do not lay eggs but give birth to live babies, suckling them with milk until the babies are able to find their own food.

Bats are the only mammals which truly fly, yet their arms and hands are very like yours and mine, so much so that long ago they were given the name *Chiroptera*, which means 'hand-wing'. Imagine if *your* four fingers were almost as long as your body, with a membrane of skin stretching between each finger and out from your side right down to your ankle. You would have 'hand-wings', very like those of a bat.

Each species or type of bat is different, flying, feeding and living in its own special way. Some species of bats have been studied much more than others, but there is still a great deal to be learnt about them all.

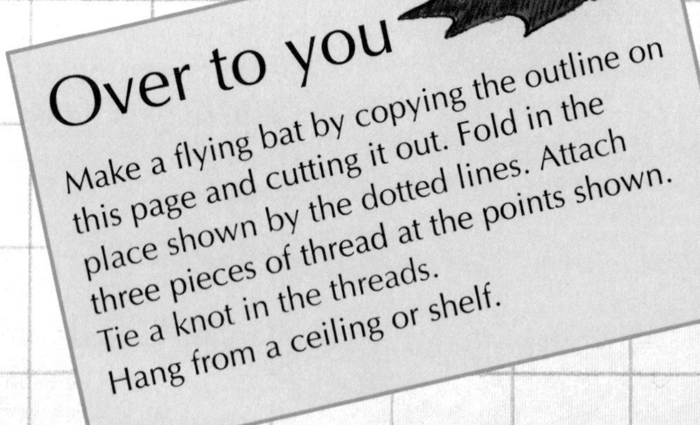

Over to you

Make a flying bat by copying the outline on this page and cutting it out. Fold in the place shown by the dotted lines. Attach three pieces of thread at the points shown. Tie a knot in the threads. Hang from a ceiling or shelf.

EARS

CUT A SLOT FOR EARS

CUT

Without realising it, we do many things that can harm bats and their **habitats** (the places they need to live and feed). Today, more and more people are finding out how fascinating bats are, and how important they are to the whole web of life on earth. Many bats are in danger of becoming extinct and only by learning more about their life-styles and needs can we plan for their conservation.

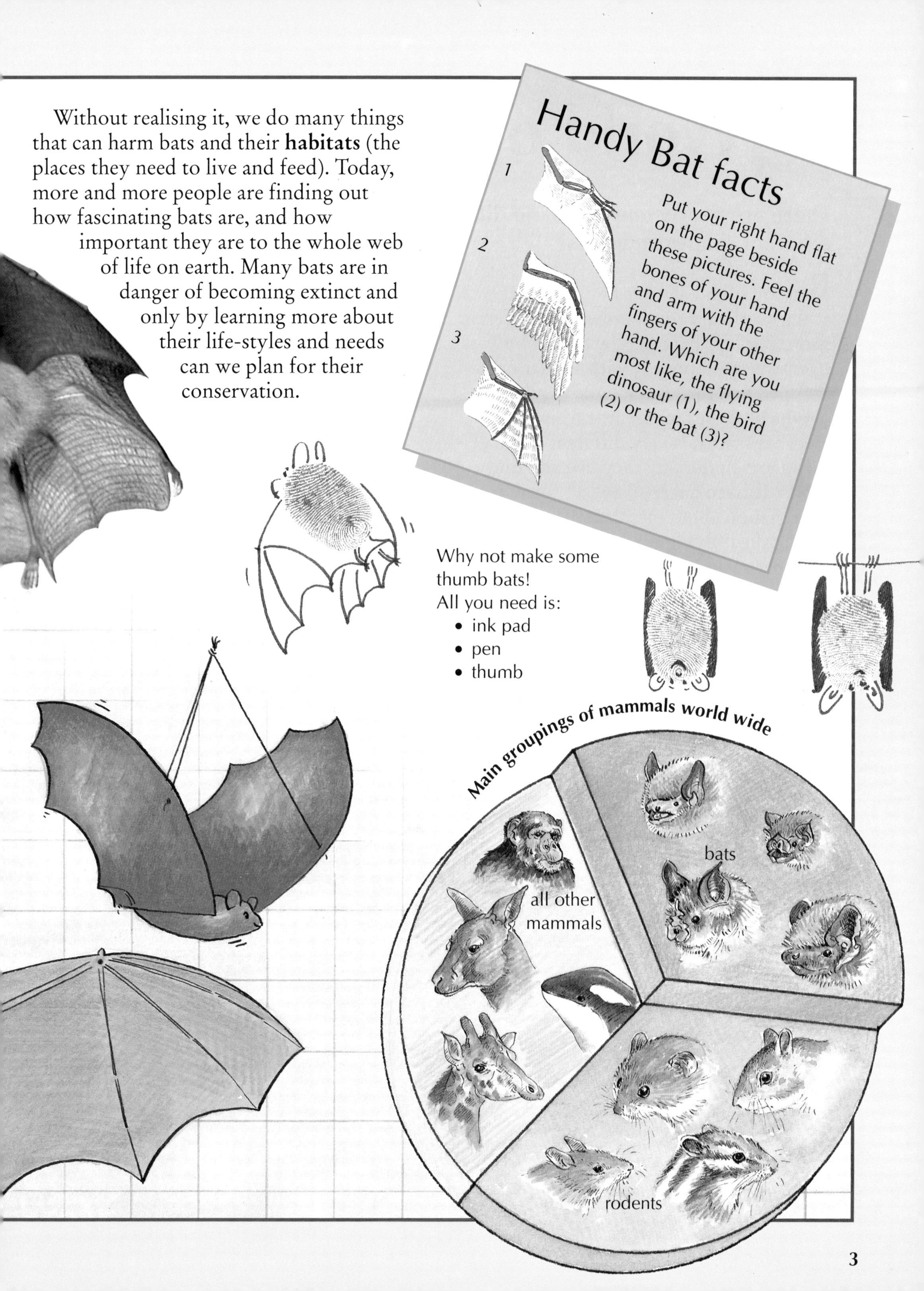

World of bats

There are nearly one thousand different types of bats of many different shapes and sizes.

Bats are found all over the world except at the north and south poles. The different species of bats have been arranged by scientists into families, with similar bats grouped together in the same families.

One of these families, the fruit bat or megabat family, is very different from all the others in the way they live and find food. (Turn to pages 10 and 11 for more information about megabats.) They are often called 'flying foxes' because of their beautiful foxy faces. All the other bat families are called microbats. They are generally smaller than megabats and have much more varied diets.

All the different bats need different sorts of foods, so more types of bats are found where the food is most varied. The greatest variety of bat species is found in the tropical areas of the world, near the equator. Fewer species are found closer to the north and south poles because it is colder there and the vegetation is less varied. More species are found on bigger areas of land than on small islands.

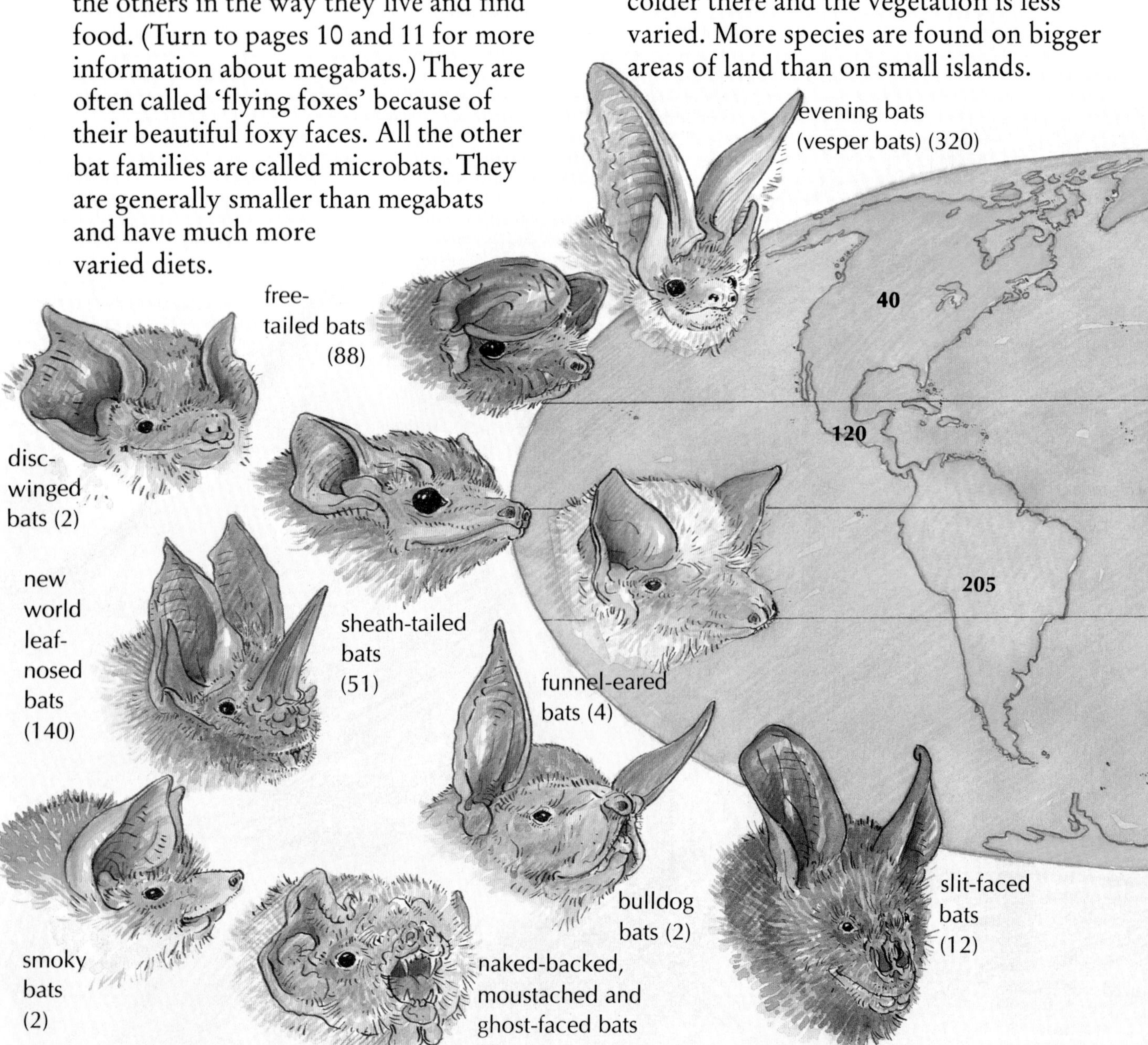

Generally, if you want to see lots of bats, keep to the big continents, keep close to the equator and find good, rich undisturbed habitats. Turn left up the Amazon, first right up a side river and the different sorts of bats awaiting you will make your head spin!

This map shows the number of different bat species which exist in each country or continent in the world. Each of the different bat families is shown around the edge of the map, with the number of species in the family in brackets.

World bat facts

- The smallest bat in the world is the bumblebee bat of Thailand weighing as little as a thimble (3 grams).
- The biggest bat in the world is a flying fox of south-east Asia, which has a 2 metre wingspan.
- Some species in south-east Asia have no fur. They're called naked bats.
- One African bat has a crest of long hair which sticks up between its ears like a punk!
- Some Central American bats are white all over.
- In New Zealand, the short-tailed bat often runs on the ground under fallen leaves looking for food.
- The male hammer-headed bats of Africa hang up and loudly 'honk' to attract females.

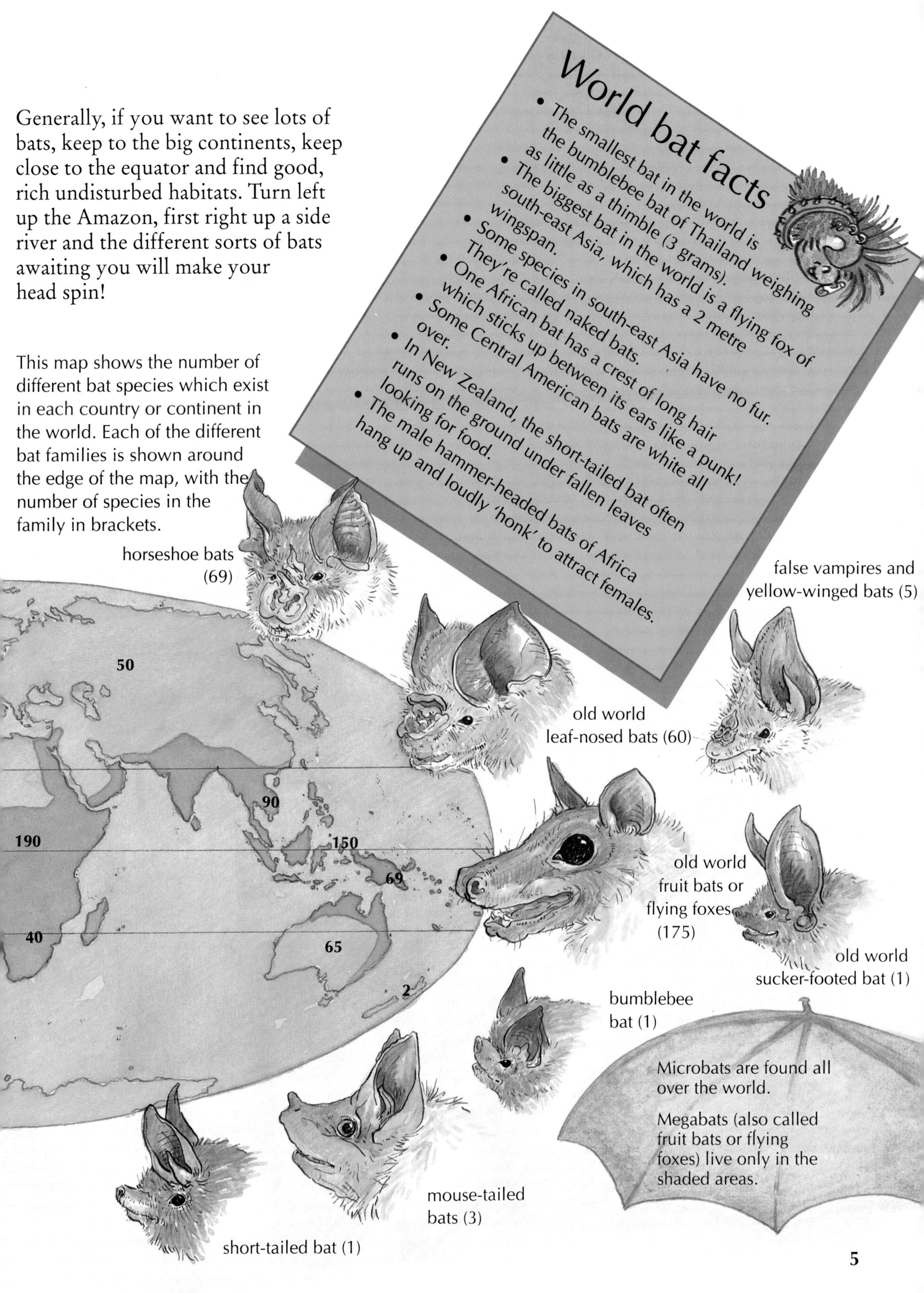

Food

Insects are by far the most popular food of microbats, but each bat species tends to eat a different mixture of what is available.

In this way, bats are less likely to compete with each other for the same food. Some will hunt high over the tops of trees where big beetles fly, others low over water where insects often sit; some around orchards where moths fly and others in gardens where those pesky mosquitoes abound. When hunting tiny insects, bats choose places where clouds of them gather and take in mouthfuls. Bigger insects are hunted individually – either chased around the sky or snatched from a leaf where they may be resting. This is, of course, one reason why different bats are designed in different ways: bats with narrow wings are fast fliers that chase flying insects, broad- winged bats often hover and can sneak up on sitting insects and pluck them off leaves.

Some bats catch other food. In tropical areas for instance, some insect-eating bats will eat fruit during part of the year.

Some bats have become specialised enough to take fish from the surface of pools; some eat frogs and lizards and some even eat smaller bats. Some microbats eat pollen, nectar and fruit just like the megabats. Perhaps the most famous food source of all bats is that of the vampire bats of South America: they feed on a small amount of blood from cattle and other animals to keep themselves alive.

CONSERVATION TIP

Plant insect-attracting flowers and shrubs – any which give out a scent at night. Fix up a night-time security light to attract thousands of insects. This way you'll provide food for bats.

Over to you

Draw bat shapes like those shown here on to folded paper. Cut them out and you can use them in all sorts of ways:

- decorate your note book cover with bat shapes.
- cut a bat carefully out of a folded circle of paper, then stick coloured tissue across the bat-shaped hole. Fasten against the window for a stained glass effect.
- fold strips of paper in a zigzag before cutting into a bat shape to make strings of bats.

Short broad-winged bats can fly slowly and may even hover.

Long narrow-winged bats are fast fliers.

Bat food facts

- The frog-eating bat of Central America finds frogs by listening for their mating calls.
- In cooler areas of the world few insects fly in winter so the bats **hibernate**. By dropping their body temperatures and using up very little energy, they can survive for months without eating.
- Some fruit bats eat 2.5 times their own body weight in fruit each night.
- A tiny bat may eat two or three thousand small insects each night.
- Nectar-feeding bats have a very long tongue with a brush-like tip.
- Bats can drink by flying low over the surface of a pond or lake and sipping water like a swallow.

Hunters in the darkness

About two-thirds of all bat species are insect eating.

In fact *all* the bats of Canada, USA, Britain and Europe eat only insects. But how do bats catch them in the dark?

- **Eyesight**
  Like all mammals, bats have eyes, and they certainly use them to see where they are flying at night, but their sight is not good enough to see fast-flying insects zooming by. So bats do not depend on their eyesight to catch food.
- **Hearing**
  All bats have very good hearing, and some with big ears listen for the faint rustling sound that insects make when they move. In this way, they can find their dinner, but not when the insects are quiet, and many insects are *very, very* quiet!
- **Smell**
  It is believed that a bat's sense of smell is good. However, insects have little smell, so not even bats can find them by sniffing them out.

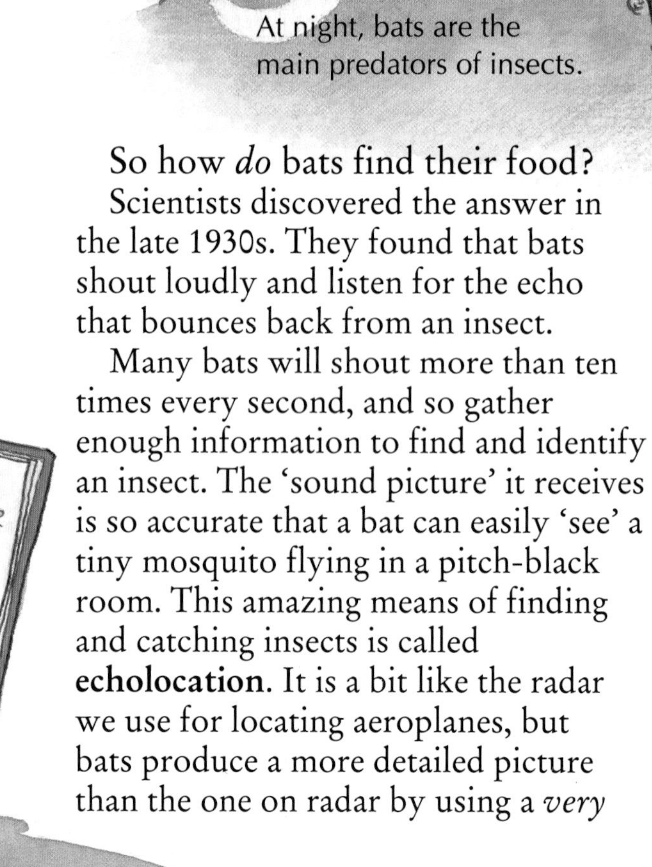

Lots of insects are caught during the day by birds using their eyesight.

At night, bats are the main predators of insects.

So how *do* bats find their food? Scientists discovered the answer in the late 1930s. They found that bats shout loudly and listen for the echo that bounces back from an insect.

Many bats will shout more than ten times every second, and so gather enough information to find and identify an insect. The 'sound picture' it receives is so accurate that a bat can easily 'see' a tiny mosquito flying in a pitch-black room. This amazing means of finding and catching insects is called **echolocation**. It is a bit like the radar we use for locating aeroplanes, but bats produce a more detailed picture than the one on radar by using a *very* high-pitched call, which is why we cannot hear them shouting as they fly around. Young people may hear part of the call, but older people rarely can. Bats' odd-shaped noses and the tragus in their ears (find it in the picture on the left) are all part of their sound system. Bats also use echolocation for finding crevices in dark caves to creep into.

- A shout goes out.
- The insect reflects back part of the sound.
- The tragus is thought to help make the sound picture clear.

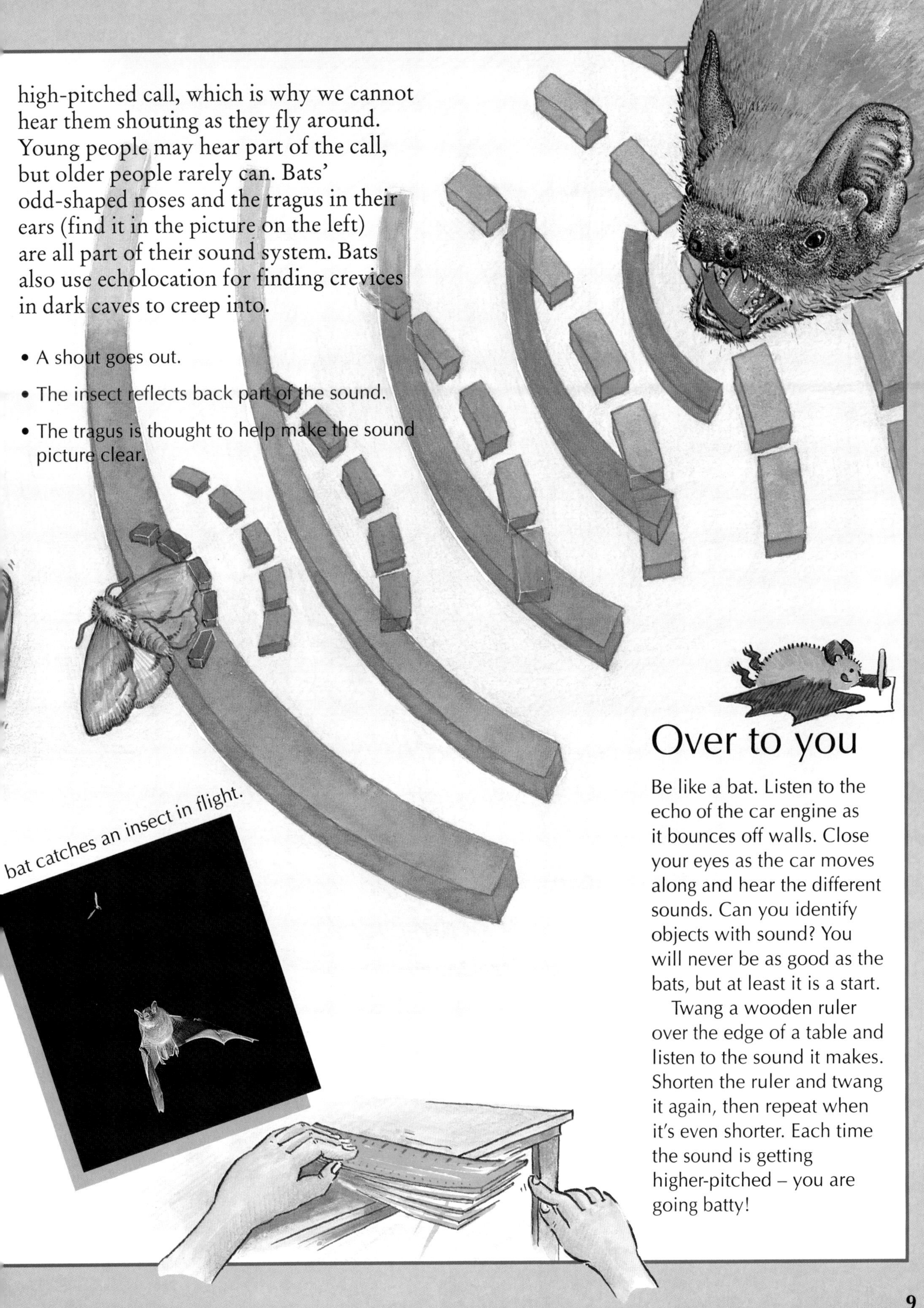

bat catches an insect in flight.

Over to you

Be like a bat. Listen to the echo of the car engine as it bounces off walls. Close your eyes as the car moves along and hear the different sounds. Can you identify objects with sound? You will never be as good as the bats, but at least it is a start.

Twang a wooden ruler over the edge of a table and listen to the sound it makes. Shorten the ruler and twang it again, then repeat when it's even shorter. Each time the sound is getting higher-pitched – you are going batty!

Giants amongst bats

Megabats are the vegetarians of the bat world, feeding on pollen and nectar as well as fruit and occasionally even on leaves.

It is easy to see why megabats' faces, often with a long muzzle, have earned them the name 'flying foxes'.

Megabats are very social creatures, living in large colonies, or camps. In parts of the tropics, many thousands can be seen hanging in the upper branches of trees during the day, chattering noisily if disturbed. When asleep, their wings can completely enclose their body.

Although they feed at night, they do not use echolocation like microbats. Their sensitive noses and large eyes enable them to follow the scent of flowers and ripe fruit and locate them even in darkness. Sometimes they travel many kilometres in search of their favourite trees. As they fly from one blossom to the next, pollen is carried on their fur, pollinating the forest trees. Those bats which eat fruit help to spread seeds in their droppings.

Most are very large, with huge wings, hence their name 'megabats'. However, there are exceptions to every rule. The little blossom bats are midgets among the giants, some with a head and body measuring only 50 mm (2 inches) long. They hover in front of a flower, their long tongues reaching deep inside to take nectar.

Over to you

Imagine you have to find your food using only your senses of smell and taste. Make a collection of different foods and experiment with a friend. Take it in turns to wear a blindfold while you test different samples.

Try: grains of salt and sugar;
cubes of margarine, butter, cheese;
slices of tomato, cucumber, courgette;
similar-shaped pieces of apple, banana, pear, grape, orange.

A grey-headed fruit bat feeds on turpentine blossom.

Identify some by smell first, then taste, and some the other way round. How many do you get right? Would you make a good megabat?

Megabat facts

- A few megabats use a simple tongue-clicking system, something like the microbats' echolocation system, to avoid colliding with the walls in their cave roosts.
- Hundreds of useful products come from plants pollinated by bats. (Have a go at the puzzle on page 29 to find out what some of these products are.)
- In cleared areas of rain forest, more than ninety per cent of the seeds scattered are dropped by bats, so planting new trees all the time.

Where bats hang up

Bats use many different places to hang up through the year. Each place they rest is known as a roost.

Where they roost depends on the time of day, the season, whether they are male or female and what part of the world they live in. Different species often prefer to roost in different places.

Whilst nearly all megabats roost in the open, most other bats tuck themselves away in cracks and crannies, or hang up under cover, especially during daylight. At night, between bouts of feeding, they use night roosts to have a break and digest their food. In general, they need somewhere warm in summer but cool in winter if they live in parts of the world where hibernation is necessary.

Flight uses a great deal of energy. In our homes we can save energy by turning down the heating, and that's just what bats do – but in their own bodies. Even in summer bats may become torpid (dormant like a hibernating animal), turning down their 'heating' by dropping their body temperatures during the day, in order to survive on less food.

In places where winters are cold, some bats migrate while others hibernate, switching off almost completely as their heart beat and breathing slow down.

Over to you

Make an amazing balancing bat. It will hang on your fingertip, the table corner, anywhere.

cork

fork

pin

Decorate your bat with wings, ears and face.

They hibernate in places which stay constantly cool, but even here they will wake to drink or feed at times, or move on to another hibernation site.

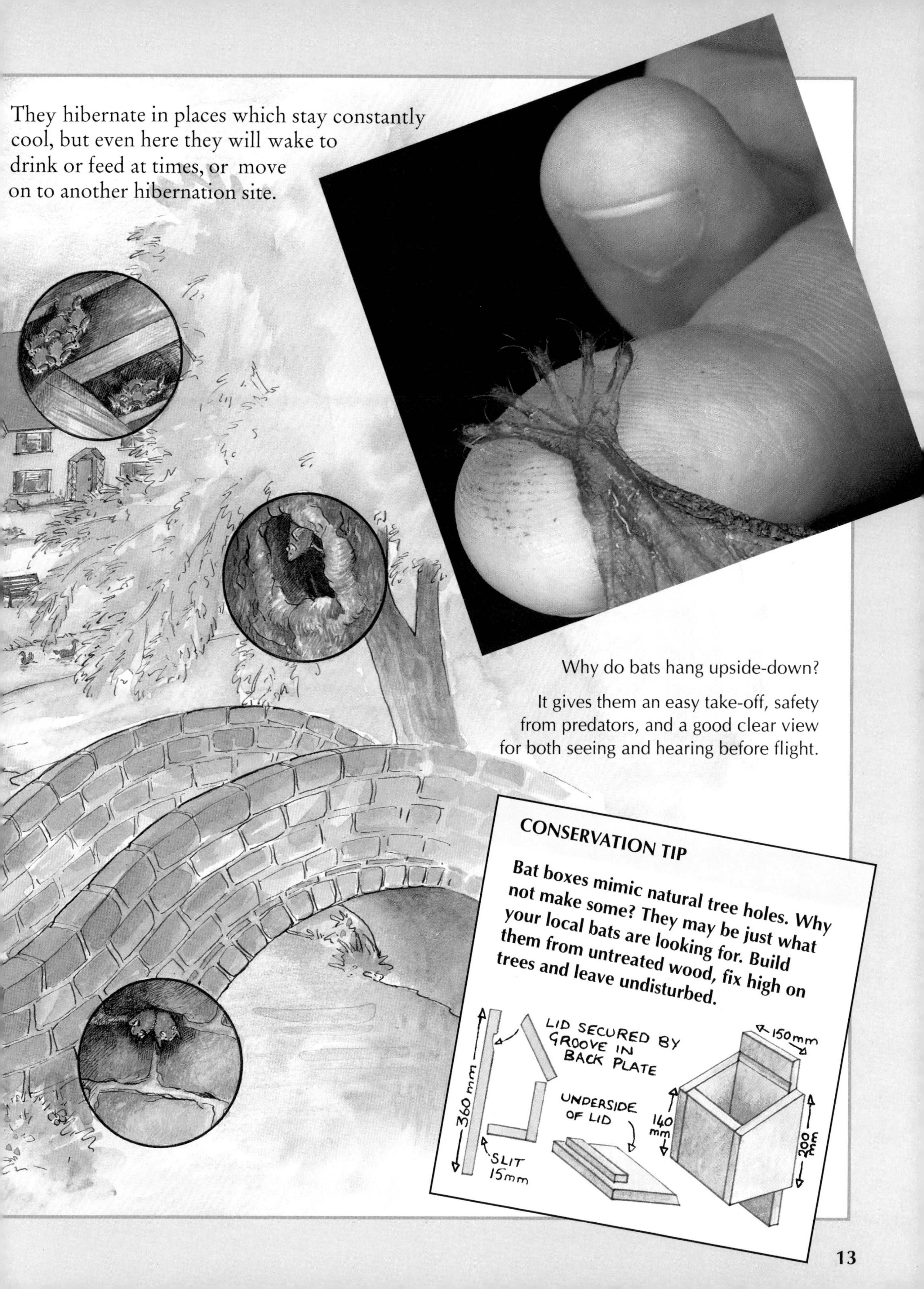

Why do bats hang upside-down?

It gives them an easy take-off, safety from predators, and a good clear view for both seeing and hearing before flight.

CONSERVATION TIP

Bat boxes mimic natural tree holes. Why not make some? They may be just what your local bats are looking for. Build them from untreated wood, fix high on trees and leave undisturbed.

Babies

A bat nursery is a bustle of constant movement.

It is important for mother bats to find a warm, safe place to have their babies, preferably near good feeding sites. These are called **maternity roosts**, and large numbers of mother bats may move into such a place in spring. Even amongst hundreds of others, a mother bat recognises her own baby by its voice and smell.

Most mammals build a nest in a safe, hidden place, some under the ground, but bats make no nest. Instead, the mother herself provides warmth and protection. As soon as the baby is born it crawls into her fur, seeking the nipple under her armpit, so the mother's wing is folded round the baby as it feeds. Tiny, hooked milk teeth enable the baby to hang on tightly, and its feet and thumbs are almost the size of an adult bat's, so it can hang up from birth. Just imagine human babies with adult feet! The baby bat is fed on milk for a few weeks to several months, depending on what sort of bat it is.

The fingers and wings of a newborn bat are only partially developed, but a baby soon starts to walk and climb, exploring the roost while its mother is away. If a baby strays too far, its mother will find it and carry it back. When taking its first flight, a baby bat does not find its own food. It is glad of its mother's milk when it returns to the maternity roost.

Young bats start to clean themselves when they are still very small. All bats spend hours grooming themselves, using their toes to comb their fur. They lick their wings carefully to keep them in good condition.

This photograph shows mothers and babies in a maternity roost.

1 Can you see a very young baby with no fur in the photograph?

2 How many babies can you find altogether?

3 How many mothers have stayed to look after the babies while the other mothers have gone to feed?

4 Compare the size of a baby bat's thumb with that of an adult.

5 Although the babies are too young to fly, look for some practising stretching their wings.

CONSERVATION TIP

Bats need to feel safe in their maternity roost. Mother and babies are easily alarmed. Never go into bat roosts, especially when young bats are there.

Baby bat facts

- Female bats often return to the same roost year after year.
- Micro-babies are born with eyes closed and without fur, though their eyes soon open.
- Mega-babies are born with fur and open eyes.
- Most bats only have one baby in a year, and not even every year.
- As in most mammal species, many baby bats die in the first few months of life, but some bats may live for over 20 years.
- Most micro-mothers usually leave their babies hanging in the roost while they go out to hunt, returning to suckle them.
- Some of the large fruit bat babies are carried to the feeding areas each night by mother until they are several weeks old, and hung up nearby while she feeds.

Over to you

A mother bat recognises her own baby by its cry.
How many voices and other sounds can you recognise with your eyes closed? Listen at school and at home.

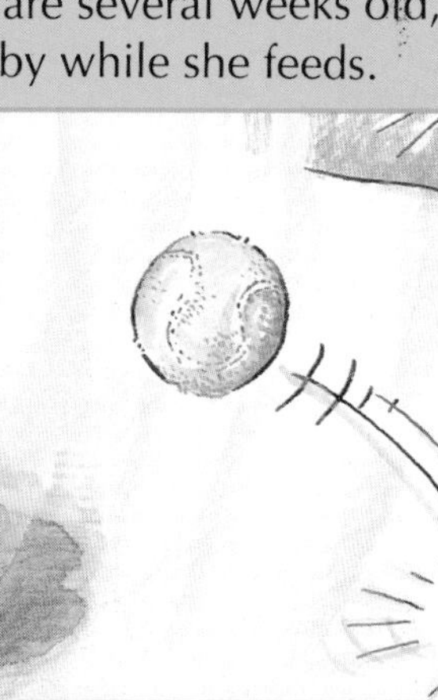

Changes

Bats were around over 50 million years ago, and fossils of bats show us their basic design remains unchanged.

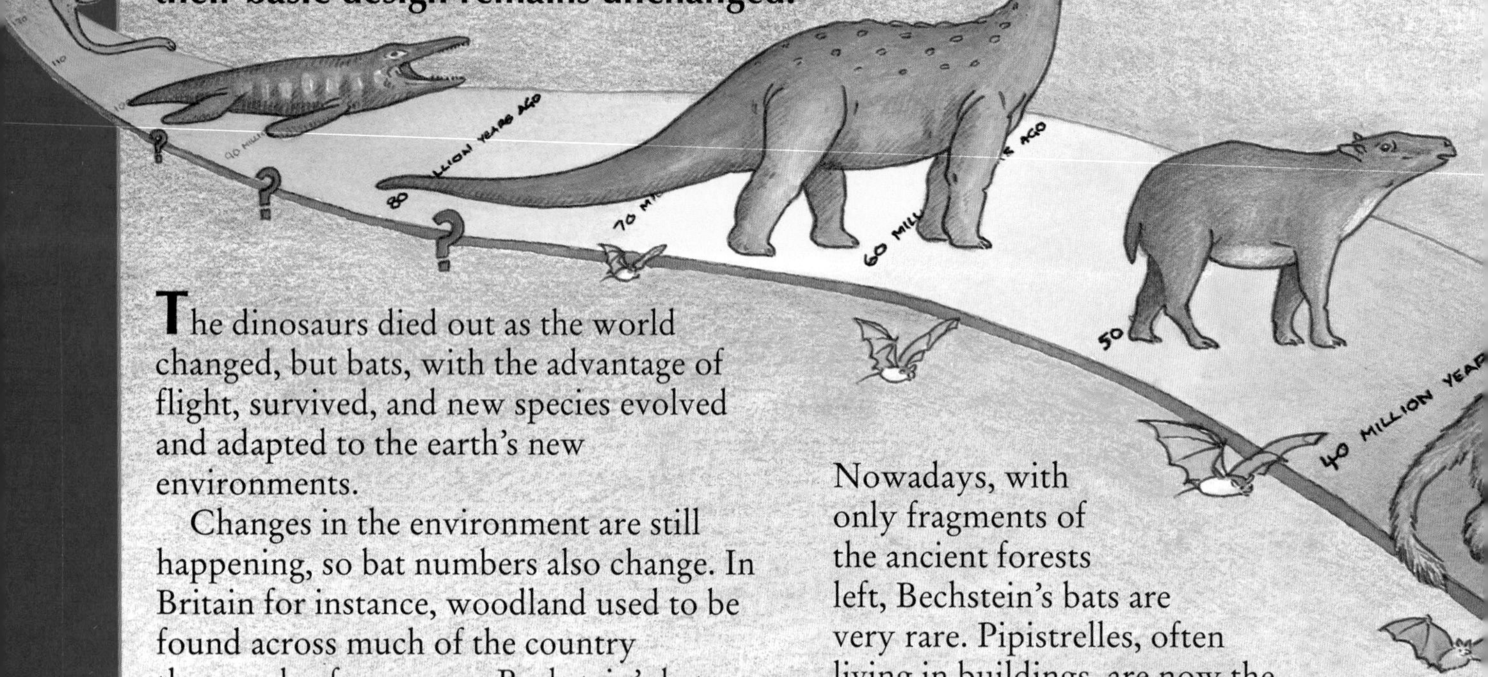

The dinosaurs died out as the world changed, but bats, with the advantage of flight, survived, and new species evolved and adapted to the earth's new environments.

Changes in the environment are still happening, so bat numbers also change. In Britain for instance, woodland used to be found across much of the country thousands of years ago. Bechstein's bat, a woodland species, seems to have been quite common then. Remains of this species are found more often in archeological digs than any other species.

Nowadays, with only fragments of the ancient forests left, Bechstein's bats are very rare. Pipistrelles, often living in buildings, are now the commonest bat by far, yet few remains of them are ever found from ancient times.

Changes can be rapid. In Israel, many fruit trees have been planted over the last few decades. The Egyptian fruit bat has now moved in, yet was unknown there before this change in agriculture.

In Central and South America there used to be few large mammals for vampire bats to feed on. When humans began to populate these areas over the last couple of centuries, they brought horses, sheep and cattle. The numbers of vampire bats increased accordingly.

This is a fossil bat set in rock which is over fifty million years old.

In Europe, Daubenton's bat is now commonly seen feeding over reservoirs, canals and flooded gravel pits which did not exist two centuries ago. This water now provides these bats with plenty of aquatic insects to feed on.

CONSERVATION TIP

Are there changes you could make or encourage to give more opportunities for feeding and roosting?

Over to you

Discover what changes to the environment have taken place in an area you know well. Look at old maps, talk to people, visit the library and museum. Take photographs, make your own sketches and maps, and compare with old ones. Has woodland or water been lost or gained? How might changes have affected bats?

Changing conditions cause species to slowly change, or **evolve**, over millions of years. Some do not change and become extinct. Some survive by moving into new areas or adapting to the changes.

Changes that help one species of bat may be disastrous for another, and many species of bat are becoming threatened with extinction as humans change the environment around them.

Bats in danger

People are now beginning to recognise that bats are in danger of dying out because of what is being done to their habitats and food supply. A Chiroptera Specialist Group (CSG) of the Species Survival Commission has been set up. It has members in all countries of the world whose task is to highlight bat conservation problems and to work out ways of overcoming them. This is often done by means of action plans for protection of habitats and roosts. Actions being undertaken include the protection of a large hibernation site in Poland and the conservation of fruit bats on tropical islands.

Bats have few natural predators.

Hawks and owls catch a few, and in some countries snakes lay in wait at cave entrances as bats emerge, but these have little impact on bat numbers. Domestic cats can be more of a problem, often catching or injuring bats as they leave their roost, or fly low to feed. However, only one animal is a real threat to bats. This species has done untold harm to bats throughout the world in recent times. The name of this species is **man**.

People have misunderstood and mistreated bats for centuries. They have hunted them for food and even sport, but the real harm has been caused by the sudden changes people have made to the environment over the last fifty years – and continue to make.

Bats need habitats which provide them with plenty of food and a wide choice of undisturbed roost sites through the year. Anything which affects either of these affects bats.

CONSERVATION TIP

Put on an exhibition or give a talk at school. Get your friends and teachers interested. Can the school grounds be improved for bats? Is there a bat conservation society you can join? See page 32 for some addresses of organisations to contact.

Black bat facts

People have:

- misunderstood bats. Campaigns against bats, wrongly believed to be pests, have killed many thousands, especially in the tropics.
- disturbed bats. Tourism, mining, and even deliberate vandalism have led to the loss of huge colonies of cave bats.
- destroyed bat homes. More wild land used up for human living space and roads means less for wildlife – and fewer roost sites for bats throughout the world.
- reduced bat food supplies, by spraying land and crops to kill insects.
- poisoned bats. Pesticides are passed on to bats through the insects that they eat. Chemicals used on the land also drain into waterways, affecting the insects living there.
- exploited bats. In some countries bats have become a delicacy for tourists to eat.
- blocked bats out of our house roofs, although they do no harm.

Over to you

1 Write a story or poem about 'The bat colony that lost its forest', or 'Looking for a mate – by a rare bat'. How could you give your story a hopeful ending?
2 Design a poster with the theme 'Bats need friends'.
3 Make and wear a bat badge to advertise your concern for bats.

Bats in Britain and the rest of Europe

In Europe, bat species become scarcer as you move northwards and westwards.

Eire
Britain
Holland
Sweden
Poland
Germany

There are thirty bat species in Western Europe, but only fourteen in Britain and seven in Eire, all of them insect-eating. The northern parts of Europe are very cold in winter, so some bats migrate in autumn to be in the warmer south for winter.

Laws protecting bats exist in most European countries, but the effect of these laws varies considerably. In some countries, few people are interested in bats, but in others, surveys are being carried out to find out more about these fascinating mammals and how they can be helped.

One of Europe's biggest bat hibernation sites is in Poland. Over 30,000 bats roost there in winter, and each year researchers count the bats carefully to see if their numbers are declining. In Sweden and Germany, bat workers drive around huge areas of countryside with bat detectors and record how many bats are feeding in each area. In Holland, bat workers are finding bat roosting sites and feeding areas by following them on bicycles using bat detectors to track the bats. In Britain, hundreds of small squares of countryside have been checked to see which habitats are best for bats. Some bats are ringed to see how long they live, others are marked and followed to see where they fly to. Roosts are counted, injured bats helped. Some people even examine bat droppings to see what insects the bats have been eating!

Organisations have been set up to protect bats and help conserve them, such as in Britain, where over eighty Bat Groups – groups of bat workers – are linked by The Bat Conservation Trust.

Over to you

Find out what laws to protect bats apply near you. What wildlife organisations work to help bats where you live? Look at the list of addresses at the back of this book to see who you should contact to find out where to start.

Bat roosting boxes are put up in areas where bats cannot find other homes.

Important cave roosts are protected from disturbance by grilles that keep people out but allow the bats in.

Bat detectors pick up the high-pitched calls of bats and turn them into a sound we can hear.

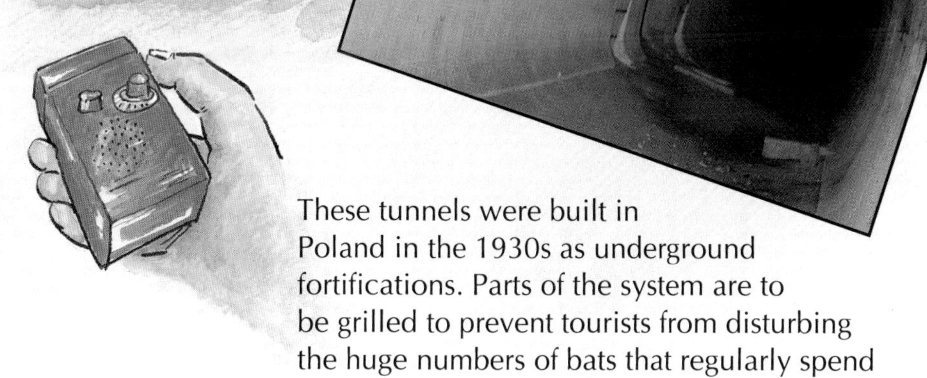

These tunnels were built in Poland in the 1930s as underground fortifications. Parts of the system are to be grilled to prevent tourists from disturbing the huge numbers of bats that regularly spend the winter here.

ropean bat facts

he smallest bat in Europe is the tiny ipistrelle. It weighs the same as 10 paperclips!

The biggest European bat, the mouse-eared bat, has a body only 7 cm (less than 4 inches) long.

- Naturalists only began to tell one bat species from another in the late 1700s, and even today some species are so similar it is hard to distinguish between them.
- Even with all the research on bats in Europe we still do not know the exact conditions needed by bats to survive.
- Horseshoe bats echolocate at frequencies six times higher than the sounds heard by humans.
- Some bats have migrated over 1000 km from northern Europe to the warmer south in winter.

The Bat Conservation Trust

The BCT is based in Britain, with membership open to everyone, including a special Junior membership. It exists to conserve bats, their roosts and habitats, by direct help, by studies and through education. Information leaflets, booklets and newsletters are produced.

The European Coordinating Panel for Bat Conservation

This is a panel of representatives of those working on bats in Europe. Results of studies are shared, and ideas produced on new ways of helping bats.

Bats in Canada and the United States of America

Only nineteen species of bat live in Canada, and some of these migrate in harsh winters into the USA where forty species can be found.

The red bat of Canada flies south in autumn following similar routes to those taken by birds. Perhaps the greatest traveller is the hoary bat. Some live in Canada and the USA for part of the year but migrate south to the tropics for the winter.

Different bats are found in different habitats – from dry deserts in New Mexico to swamps in Mississippi and from mountain ranges to prairies. The yellow bat only lives in the extreme south and often roosts under the fronds of palms which grow there. The pallid bat feeds on scorpions and grasshoppers on the ground and prefers the dry areas. It is thought it can hear the pitter-patter of scorpion feet and thus locate its prey.

Bats have only limited protection by law in the USA and Canada, and roost entrances may be blocked. Habitats in the huge National Parks are protected, but bats in buildings are still at risk. The Canadian and American people are becoming more aware of the need to conserve bats and attitudes towards them are changing – caves are protected, house-roosts are studied, surveys are being done.

CONSERVATION TIP

Write a letter for your neighbourhood newspaper, or a magazine, about improving the environment for bats. Letters can help if there are enough of them, so get your friends to write too or add their signatures.

Over to you

Give a Batty Party for Hallowe'en, Christmas, a birthday or other celebrations. Serve bat-shaped biscuits and cakes, bat salad, put up batty decorations and play batty games. Send batty cards at these times – make them friendly bats!

Bat Conservation International
This is an international organisation which helps fund public education, research and conservation of threatened and endangered bats. It produces slide packs, information and videos to help conserve bats of the world.

American Bat Conservation Society
This society conserves bats through direct action, educational programmes and field studies. It also helps injured and orphaned bats.

Mexican Free-Tailed Bats

The Mexican free-tailed bat which lives in the USA occupies only ten or so caves, yet the numbers of these bats are staggering. Bracken Cave in Texas has held 20 million Mexican free-tailed bats in the past, which must be the world's highest concentration of mammals! They stream out of the cave at dusk at a great rate, giving tourists a sight never to be forgotten. These bats are believed to fly over 70 kms to feeding areas before returning just before dawn and plunging at terrific speed back into their cave. The Mexican free-tailed bat is one of the faster flying bats of the world, and the wind over its wings can make an exciting whistling sound.

BCI

Numbers of free-tailed bats in recent years have fallen dramatically, and the use of insect poisons is believed to have been one cause of their decline. Bats eating poisoned insects become weak and die.

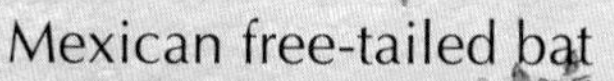
Mexican free-tailed bat

Bats in Central and South America

Amazon

Brazil

Now we are in the hot, humid tropics, full of hot, humid jungles. The types of insects and plants here are too many to list.

Some of the world's prettiest bats live in this remote part of the world, and there are more species of bat here than anywhere else.

There are no megabats like those in Africa or Australia, but since there are lots of fruits some microbats have evolved to eat them – and pollen and nectar and fish and frogs and lizards and even blood! You name it and there will be a bat adapted to eat it or live under it – like banana leaves, which the tent-making bat nibbles to make the leaves droop down to provide shelter from the tropical rain!

Other bats have stripes, funny-shaped faces, some are long-nosed and others are big-eared. Species of bat probably exist in this incredibly rich area for wildlife. which haven't yet been discovered. Many live in old, hollow trees and deep in caves – these are the first places to look next time you are canoeing up the Amazon! But be quick. The wonderful rain forests that are home to these spectacular bats and other amazing creatures are being chopped down at an alarming rate, and that means the bats will have nowhere to live and nowhere to feed. Unfortunately, few of the countries in this region have any laws that protect the bats or their habitats.

Vampires

The vampire bat is not a monster-bat, but actually less than 100 mm (4 inches) long! Three species of vampire bat exist, but two of these are so rare that few people ever see them. All live on small amounts of blood taken from small animals, birds or cattle and horses. Very occasionally they have been known to take blood from humans, but the amount of blood given by a blood donor would keep one vampire well-fed for a month!

Over to you

Use an atlas to find out which other countries are part of South and Central America. Try to discover more about them and the many bats that are found there and nowhere else.

The large feet and claws on the long legs of the fisherman bat are used to snatch small fish from the surface of water. When the fishing is no good, they eat insects.

Odd folds and wrinkles make the wrinkle-faced bat look rather peculiar. It is sometimes called the 'old man bat.'

Logging has destroyed magnificent rainforests around the globe. Many bats are endangered as a result, together with countless other wildlife species.

CONSERVATION TIP

Help save the tropical rainforest, and so protect bats and other creatures. Some organisations have made it possible for you to 'buy' a patch of rainforest. The address of one is on page 32.

Bats in Australia

Northern Territory
Cape York
Queensland
Sydney

The Ghost Bat

The territory of a ghost bat colony in Queensland was made a National Park in 1990, sadly too late to prevent several important wintering caves being blown up by a cement company mining for limestone. ghost bats in the Northern Territory are now also threatened by mining. With a wing-span of about 60 cms, the ghost bat is one of the largest carnivorous bats in the world.

About sixty-five species of bat live in Australia, including eight fruit bats.

Two-thirds of the species are found at Cape York, Australia's most north-easterly tip. Travelling south and west fewer different bats are to be found, though some even live in the dry desert areas.

Since the first European settlement 200 years ago, the Australian landscape has altered dramatically, and the habitat needed by bats for roosting, feeding and foraging drastically reduced. Large areas of forest have been cleared to make way for houses, industry, and agricultural development, growing crops such as sugar cane, pineapple and bananas.

If native trees have a poor flowering season, fruit bats may raid the orchards planted in what were originally their traditional feeding-grounds. Legal protection of bats varies between states, and in the past many bats were shot. Today, ways of protecting orchards with netting on frames, and other deterrents to bats, are being developed.

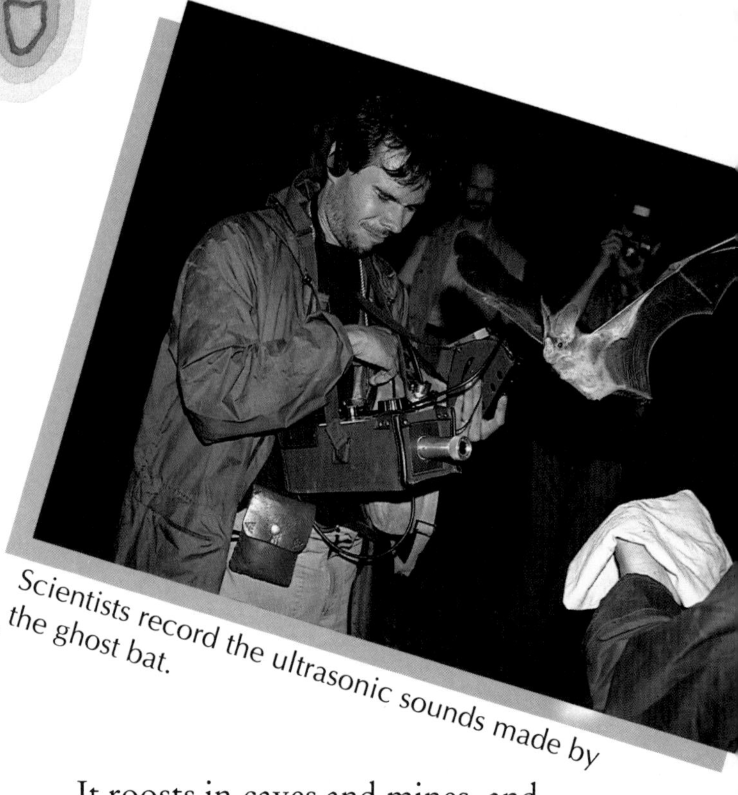

Scientists record the ultrasonic sounds made by the ghost bat.

It roosts in caves and mines, and eats many different foods including lizards, birds, beetles and even other bats! It is very shy, and easily disturbed. Scientists are radio-tracking some of these very rare animals to find out more about their needs, in order to conserve them.

CONSERVATION TIP

Mining and quarrying is destroying many cave roosts, to give us more roads, bigger houses and more luxury goods. Do we need these things? Think about our way of life, and what damage it is doing to the environment. Is it worth it?

Talks given to local children and adults help them to learn more about these beautiful animals. Places like this must be conserved if the bats are to survive.

Surburban Bats

A forested valley in the Sydney suburb of Gordon is home to a large maternity colony of grey-headed flying foxes. In 1985, the Gordon site land was bought to safeguard it from urban development, but it was still threatened by weeds which were killing the native trees.

Conservationists now remove weeds, plant native seedlings and encourage natural regrowth of trees, so providing roost trees for flying foxes in the future. The Ku-rin-gai Flying Fox Reserve is protected by a Conservation Agreement between the local Council and the State Minister of the Environment.

Over to you

Make a bobbing bat band! Cut 3 strips of stiff paper. Cut two bat shapes and crease along the fingers. Clip together as shown.

Island bats

Because of their ability to fly, bats are the only mammals to have reached some parts of the world.

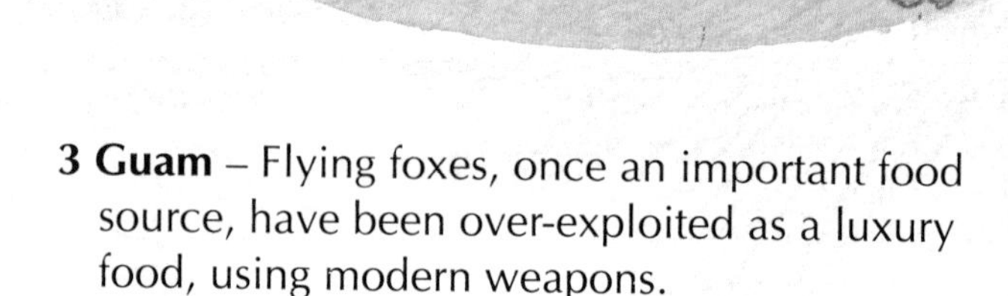

1 Comoro Islands – Livingstone's fruit bat depends on mountain forests which are being destroyed.

2 Pemba – Wet tropical forests where the bats live have been cleared for agriculture.

3 Guam – Flying foxes, once an important food source, have been over-exploited as a luxury food, using modern weapons.

4 Samoa – In 1991 cyclones devastated roosting and feeding sites. An estimated 30 per cent of the forest here depends on the bats. Two large areas of rain forest have now been saved from logging and set up as reserves for Samoan flying foxes.

5 Ulithi – a tiny atoll, 4 square kilometres, is home to an endemic (found nowhere else) sub-species of flying fox. If the colony dies out there is none elsewhere to replace it.

Bat conservation programmes are now being set up in the Indian and Pacific ocean areas.

In very remote areas these bats have gradually changed and evolved, and some kinds of flying foxes exist on a number of islands in the tropics that are found nowhere else in the world.

On many of these islands, the part bats play in pollinating flowers and spreading seeds is so important that they are known as **keystone species**. On some islands, only bats are capable of carrying some of the large-seeded fruit. If there were no bats to spread these seeds, not only would the plants die out, but so would the animals that depend on them, and those that depend on *them*.

Numbers of bats are usually not very large on small islands, so they can easily be wiped out. Although extinction may result from natural disasters, they are put even more at risk by people, both by what they do to the bats themselves and also by what they do to their habitats. In many places, forests and mangrove swamps are cleared for the wood-chipping industry, for firewood and for building development. Roads make it easier to reach the bats, unsettling them, especially groups with babies. The bats can also be more easily hunted for food or sport.

n arch is
d from
pse by its keystone, so
sland forests depend on bats.

Rodrigues Fruit Bat

The Rodrigues fruit bat is one of the rarest bats in the world. It lives in one part of Rodrigues Island, in the western Indian Ocean. It weighs up to 450 grams, and has a wingspan of up to 750 mm. It eats fruit, nectar and probably foliage. In 1976, only 130 of these bats were believed to exist. Ten bats were taken to Jersey in the Channel Islands and a captive breeding programme was set up by the Jersey Wildlife Preservation Trust. It has been so successful that the release of these bats back into the wild is being planned.

Island bat facts

- a third of all flying fox species are found in the Pacific region.
- one species, the Guam flying fox, has recently become extinct.
- several other species are close to extinction.
- many could become extinct if any disaster hit an island, and the forests cannot survive without the bats.

Over to you

AAANNSB BOARC SAALB ILALNVA SEWSHAC EATSD LASIS GFSI LSCEOV KKOAP MUGGWCEINH AAUVSG DSMOLNA MOAGNSE SADAOCVO

Can you unjumble these fifteen things that come from plants visited by bats? You will find the answers on page 32.

Find out what part of the plant each is, and what it is used for. Make a bat salad of fruit and nuts for your family to enjoy.

Bats everywhere

Bats have been used throughout the world as a powerful image in folklore, poetry and art.

Seen dimly only at dusk, with strange powers enabling them to fly and feed in total darkness, bats used to be thought to have magical qualities. Myths and strange stories came into being, and in many countries bats became symbols – sometimes of good, sometimes of evil.

Bats in folklore

Fables were invented to explain creatures that seemed to be neither beast nor bird. In many, the bat pretended to be first one, then the other, in order to have the best of both worlds, so was banished to the night for his deception.

Some Finnish people believed the soul to be freed from the body during sleep, often appearing as a bat – explaining why bats are seen only at night when people are sleeping.

Bats as symbols of good

In China the word for bat is *fu*, which is also the name of the character for 'happiness', and came to be used as a symbol of good luck. Artists still use a traditional design of five bats arranged round the tree of life to represent five blessings.

Bats as symbols of evil

As creatures of the night, bats were sometimes seen as symbolic of the darker side of life. In European paintings, good was often represented by angels with feathered wings, while devils and dragons bore leather bat-like wings.

Bats in coats-of-arms and logos

Bats have been included in many coats-of-arms of families, towns and even regiments. Sometimes this is part of a play on words, as in the Bateson family, or the bats may symbolise a certain characteristic, as in badges of a number of airforce squadrons.

Bats as charms or ingredients in potions

It was once believed that the qualities of an animal could be passed on by using it in a portion or as a charm. Potions including parts of a bat were used to improve watchfulness, wakefulness and seeing in the dark. Some were to prevent eye disease, and others to cause blindness. In some places they were used as a cure for baldness, but elsewhere to remove unwanted hair.

CONSERVATION TIP

Help conserve bats by helping to change attitudes.
Work out 20 questions about bats and attitudes to them. For example, are they blind? How many species are there? Do you like them? Test your friends and families. Put them right.
Watch for bad bat images in advertising (they still happen) and write and complain.

Vampires

There is little mention of vampires in the folklore of tropical America, the very place you would expect it, being the home of vampire bats. The story of Dracula, by Bram Stoker, was first published in 1897. In it he drew on eastern European legends about restless souls of the dead and linked them with the discovery of vampire bats by Europeans in South America.

Bats as gods

The Mayas of Central America showed a bat god on their sculptures with bat-like wings and a nose-leaf. He was believed to rule caverns and the realm of darkness. Navajo Indians in the south west desert of the USA believed bats to be a link between gods and people, offering humans helpful guidance.

Bats in rhyme

Twinkle twinkle little bat!
How I wonder what you're at!
Up above the world you fly
Like a teatray in the sky.

Lewis Carroll

Over to you

1. Can you finish this batty limerick which begins –
   There once was a young bat called Joe . . .
2. Make a bat collection of poems, stories and images of bats in art. Look in museums and art galleries as well as books.

Mythical bat facts

Even today some people have the wrong ideas about bats. How many of these myths and predjudices do you recognise?

- Blind as a bat? All bats can see!
- Flying mice? Bats are more closely related to humans than to mice!
- They get in your hair? That is the last thing they want to do!
- Bats are dirty? They are very clean animals, spending hours grooming themselves thoroughly.

Index

British Library Cataloguing in Publication Data

Thompson, Shirley A.
Bat Conservation Project Book
I. Title
599.4

ISBN 0-340-57256-6

First published 1993

Typeset by Litho Link Ltd, Welshpool, Powys, Wales.
Printed in Hong Kong for the educational publishing division of Hodder & Stoughton Ltd, Mill Road, Dunton Green, Sevenoaks, Kent by Colorcraft Ltd.

Sources of information

The Bat Conservation Trust, c/o **The Conservation Foundation, 1 Kensington Gore. London SW7 2AB**
The BCT is the UK's only organisation wholly concerned with bat conservation. A youth section operates. It produces information for both adults and children, including a free newsletter, *The Young Batworker* and can give details of your local bat group.

English Nature, Northminster Houses, Peterborough PE1 1UA.

Countryside Commission for Wales, Plas Penrhos, Ffordd, Penrhos, Bangor, Gwynedd LL57 2LQ

Scottish Natural Heritage, 12 Hope Terrace, Edinburgh EH9 2AS

The above three are the UK Government's nature conservation agencies. The appropriate one should be consulted before making changes to roost sites in the UK. Information leaflets are available.

R.S.N.C. The Wildlife Trusts Partnership, The Green, Witham Park, Waterside South, Lincoln LN5 7JR.
The national body for the County Wildlife Trusts and Urban Wildife Groups in the UK. Many bat groups are closely associated with these trusts.

WATCH, The Green, Witham Park, Waterside South, Lincoln LN5 7JR.
A junior wildlife and environment club for young people, the junior section of RSNC. There are a number of WATCH groups around the country.

Programme for Belize, P.O. Box 99 Saxmundham IP17 2LB.
Enables you to buy an acre of rainforest to save from destruction.

Always send a stamped, self-addressed envelope when writing to any organisation.

Answers to puzzle on page 29
BANANAS, CAROB, BALSA, VANILLA, CASHEWS, DATES, SISAL, FIGS, CLOVES, KAPOK, CHEWING GUM, GUAVAS, ALMONDS, MANGOES, AVOCADOS.

The authors and publishers would like to thank the following for permission to reproduce photographs in this book: Stephen Dalton NHPA, cover: Frank Greenaway pp. 2-3, 9, 13, 16, 29: National Museum & Galleries of Merseyside p. 31: Pat Morris p. 10: Phil Richardson p. 21: Hans-Peter Stutz pp. 14-15: Harold Taylor/Natural History Museum p.25: Shirley Thompson p.26: David Williams p.11